JUNGLE ANIMALS
AROUND THE WORLD

A⁺

Smart Apple Media

Published by Smart Apple Media, an imprint of Black Rabbit Books
P.O. Box 3263, Mankato, Minnesota 56002
www.blackrabbitbooks.com

Library of Congress Cataloging-in-Publication Data

Alderton, David, 1956- author.
 Jungle animals around the world / contributing authors, David Alderton [and nine others] / consulting editor,
Per Christiansen ; series editor, Sarah Uttridge.
    pages cm. -- (Animals around the world)
 Audience: Grades 4 to 6.
 Includes index.
 ISBN 978-1-62588-194-6
1. Jungle animals--Juvenile literature. 2. Jungles--Juvenile literature. I. Christiansen, Per, editor. II. Uttridge,
Sarah, editor. III. Title.
 QL112.A385 2015
 591.734--dc23
                        2013042512

Contributing Authors: David Alderton, Susan Barraclough, Per Christiansen, Kieron Connolly,
Paula Hammond, Tom Jackson, Claudia Martin, Carl Mehling, Veronica Ross, Sarah Uttridge
Consulting Editor: Per Christiansen
Series Editor: Sarah Uttridge
Editorial Assistant: Kieron Connolly
Designer: Andrew Easton
Picture Research: Terry Forshaw

Printed in the United States at Corporate Graphics, Mankato, Minnesota,
4-2014
PO 1650
9 8 7 6 5 4 3 2 1

Photo Credits:
Dreamstime: 1 Eric Gevaert, 4, 21t Minyun Zhou, 7l Andrey Kuzmin,
7r Roman Milert, 9t Duncan Noakes, 9b Charles Sichel-Outcalt, 12/13
Nichapa329, 12t Vukpiper, 12b Cafea, 15t Seeingimages, 17t Saroj007,
17b Cheng Zhong, 19l Sunheyy, 19r Anthony Hathaway, 25l Timothy
Lubcke, 25r Robert Bayer, 29l Vilaincrevette, front cover; **FLPA:** 6/7
Patricio Robles Gil, 8/9, 14/15 David Hosking, 10/11 Tim Fitzharris, 16/17
Sergey Gorshkov, 20/21 Jurgen & Christine Sohns, 22/23 Christian
Ziegler, 24/25 Reinhard Dirscherl, 26/27, 27l Wil Meinderts, 27r Bruno
Cavinaux/Biosphoto; **Photos.com:** 21b; **Shutterstock:** 11l Stephen
Bonk, 11r Audrey Snider-Bell, 15b Javarman, 23 both Dirk Ercken, 29r
Kjersti Joergensen.

Contents

Introduction

The jungles on our planet are full of wild animals that vary in how they look, where they live, and what they eat. About half of all the animal species on Earth—mammals, birds, insects, amphibians, and reptiles—live in the jungle. Many species of jungle animals are endangered. Others have become extinct as the amount of rain forest on the planet is destroyed.

Asian Elephant

These are the largest land mammals in Asia. They live in family-based herds led by the eldest female. Because they are so big and because their digestion is poor, they have to eat huge quantities of plants every day to survive. They can live for up to 70 years.

WHERE DO THEY LIVE?

They live in isolated regions in India, Sri Lanka, Malaysia, Indonesia, and China.

Asia

Feet Pads

▶ The foot contains soft, fatty pads, allowing the elephant to leave only light tracks and move almost silently.

DID YOU KNOW?

 They can swim well and use their trunk like a snorkel to allow them to breathe underwater.

 The African elephant is about 20 percent larger than the Asian elephant.

 The Asian elephant's skull takes up 25 percent of its body weight.

FACTS

SIZE

● Females are 7–8 ft. (2.1–2.4 m) tall, males up to 10 ft. (3 m).

● It once ranged from Iraq to northern China.

● It has a twin-domed forehead, unlike the African elephant.

Flapping Ears

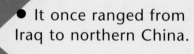 The ears of the Asian elephant are smaller than those of the African elephant. The undersides of the ears have many blood vessels that can carry the heat from the body to the ears. When the elephant flaps its ears, it can let the heat escape and keep cool.

Tusks & Teeth

◀ Most males and a few females have tusks, which are developed incisor teeth. It has 24 cheek teeth that are pushed out by new teeth when they wear out.

8

Crowned Eagle

This is Africa's most powerful and ferocious eagle. It mainly eats mammals, such as small antelopes and monkeys. When food is very scarce an adult crowned eagle will resort to eating birds, such as herons and storks, and reptiles, such as monitor lizards and snakes.

WHERE DO THEY LIVE?

Africa

Dense forests in Uganda, Kenya, Congo, Zambia, Zimbabwe, and South Africa.

Crest

▶ The large crest is often raised. The bird's large size makes it easy to recognize when seen up close.

Color

◄ The crowned eagle has dark gray upper parts with reddish-brown and white below. Its belly and breast are heavily mottled with black.

FACTS

SIZE

- This eagle can carry a weight equal to its own body weight: 6.5–13 lbs. (3–6 kg).

- The crowned eagle can attack animals that weigh up to 66 lbs. (30 kg).

DID YOU KNOW?

 As with most birds of prey, the female is larger than the male.

 The crowned eagle will only travel 4–10 miles (6.4–16 km) to hunt for prey.

 It will usually kill using its talons, but can also kill by squeezing its prey tight and stopping it from breathing.

Eagle Nests

▶ Crowned eagle pairs breed once every two years. A male and female crowned eagle work together to build a nest in the fork between a branch and the trunk of a large tree. The nest can be up to 8 ft. (2.5 m) across and 9.8 ft. (3 m) deep. The nest is made from both dead and greener branches. A new nest can take up to five months to build, but older nests can be repaired and reused more quickly.

Emerald Tree Boa

This snake is active during the night and lives in trees. During the day it is coiled over a tree branch with its head perched at the center. At night, it extends its head downward. It will stay in this position until prey approaches. It grabs the prey with its teeth, coils around it, and stops it from breathing.

Constrictors

▶ All boas are constrictors. This means they coil around animals, stopping them from breathing, to kill them.

WHERE DO THEY LIVE?

They are found in South America in the Amazon Basin.

South America

DID YOU KNOW?

 It looks similar to the green tree python, but in fact they are only distant relatives in the snake world.

 Boas are not a venomous snake, which means they are not poisonous.

 Millions of years ago boas and other snakes had legs like lizards.

FACTS

- Adults grow to 6 ft. (1.8 m) long.

- It has a white zigzag stripe down its back.

- After eating a large animal, the snake doesn't need any food for a long time.

SIZE

Newborns

▶ Newborns are red or orange and take a year to change to emerald green. An adult female will give birth to between six and 14 in each litter. In comparison with the size of the animal, its teeth are very big.

Feeding

◀ Its body processes food very slowly, so it only needs to eat every few months. It mainly eats small mammals. Young boas also eat birds, lizards, and frogs.

Hippo

The hippopotamus has a big, bulky body and short, stocky legs. Its short legs make it awkward on land, but it is graceful and at ease in the water. Hippos spend the day resting in water with their heads just above the surface. They are surprisingly aggressive animals and can injure or even kill people.

WHERE DO THEY LIVE?

Sahara Desert

Africa

In Africa, south of the Sahara Desert, usually close to rivers and lakes.

Water Lover

▶ Hippos spend more than 18 hours a day in the water. They only come out at night to feed on grass.

Thick Skin

◀ Hippos have sensitive skin that will crack if they spend too long in the sunshine. Their thick skin produces a pink, oily fluid to help keep the skin moist.

FACTS

SIZE

● Baby hippos are born underwater.

● Hippos' toes are webbed, which helps them paddle in water.

● Their main predators are humans.

DID YOU KNOW?

 Their huge teeth can cause serious damage to predators.

 Young hippopotamuses may rest on their mothers' shoulders, if the water is too deep for them to stand up in.

 The huge jaws can open to an angle of 150°.

Good Swimmers

▶ Hippos can stay under the water for six minutes, walking along the bottom. Their broad feet make excellent paddles for swimming. The nostrils are big but the hippo can close the openings with skin flaps when it is underwater. The eyes are also closed when under the water.

Indian Flying Fox

The Indian flying fox bat is a huge member of the bat species. Its body can be up to 12 in. (30 cm) long. Its wingspan can be 50 in. (127 cm). It feeds only on fruit such as mangoes, bananas, guavas, and figs. It uses sight and smell to find ripe fruit.

Roosting

▶ The back feet each have five digits. These have sharp claws so they can grasp branches when roosting.

WHERE DO THEY LIVE?

Europe, North Africa, and western Asia.

Europe

Asia

Africa

Furry Muzzle

◀ The head of the flying fox is furry with a foxlike muzzle. The eyes are large. This bat finds its way in the dark using only its eyesight.

FACTS

SIZE

- There are about 1,240 different bat species.

- Thick fur helps keep the bat warm.

- They live in large colonies called camps.

DID YOU KNOW?

It feeds on juice from tree fruit. It can fly over 30 miles (48 km) to find ripe fruit.

The wings are broad and very powerful. They allow the bat to travel long distances when looking for food.

Newborn flying foxes are well developed. They have lots of fur and their eyes are open.

Roost Sites

▶ The camps of flying foxes may contain several thousand bats. They take over whole trees, stripping off the leaves as they move around the branches. These roost sites may be used by many generations. The offspring of the flying foxes are born feet first. The young are carried by their mother when she goes looking for food, sometimes over 30 miles (48 km) away.

Leopard

The leopard is a deadly hunter that hides in the darkness at night before pouncing on its victims. It once ranged from Siberia to South Africa. Now it is mainly found in sub-Saharan Africa, India, and parts of Southeast Asia. Its range has decreased because of hunting and loss of habitat.

WHERE DO THEY LIVE?

Sub-Saharan Africa, India, and parts of Southeast Asia.

Sahara Desert

Asia

Africa

Daytime Rest

▶ Leopards are good at climbing, and have been observed resting on tree branches during the day.

Night Hunter

◀ The pattern on the coat hides the leopard when it rests during the day and provides camouflage while it hunts in the dim light at night.

FACTS

SIZE

- It has very sensitive whiskers on the muzzle.

- Its night vision may be six times better than that of humans.

- It can be found in a range of environments.

DID YOU KNOW?

 The leopard walks silently on its padded paws when hunting its prey.

 The female cares for a litter of two to four cubs. They stay with her for up to two years.

 To keep its food from being eaten by other animals, the leopard drags bodies of dead animals up into the branches of trees.

Coat Pattern

▶ The coat has a pale yellow to reddish-brown background with dark-rimmed, pale-centered rosettes that cover the body. The tail is ringed with black and the underparts are white. Coat patterns and color vary depending on which region the leopard is from.

Macaw

Macaws are New World parrots that can be small or large. Most species live in forests, especially rain forests, but some can be found in grassland habitats. They have large, dark beaks and bare, light-colored faces. The pattern on each macaw's face is like a human fingerprint: no two macaws have the same face pattern.

WHERE DO THEY LIVE?

Macaws are native to Mexico, Central America, and South America.

Central America

South America

Toes

▶ Their first and fourth toes point backward, like other parrots and also woodpeckers.

DID YOU KNOW?

 Macaws make lots of different sounds. Like parrots, they can copy human speech.

 The blue-and-yellow macaw has a special throat pouch that can carry extra food.

 The largest parrot in length and wingspan is the hyacinth macaw.

FACTS

SIZE

● They can live for up to 50 years.

● Most macaws are now endangered in the wild. There were 18 species of macaw, but six are now extinct.

Diet

◀ Macaws eat palm fruits, nuts, seeds, leaves, flowers, and stems. Some foods eaten by macaws in the wild contain toxic or caustic substances that they are able to digest. They also eat clay; it has been suggested that this is because they need the sodium found in the clay.

Hooked Bill

◀ The hooked bill is strong enough to crack through the outer shells of rain forest seeds. The bird grinds the seed between its upper and lower mouth parts.

Orangutan

Orangutans are the only great apes that are only found in Asia. Of all the great apes (chimps, gorillas, bonobos), orangutans spend the most time in trees. Unlike the black-haired African apes, orangutans have reddish-brown hair. They are the most solitary of the great apes, with the strongest bonds between mothers and their offspring.

WHERE DO THEY LIVE?

Orangutans are found only in the rain forests of Borneo and Sumatra in Southeast Asia.

Asia

Males

◀ Dominant adult males have large cheek pads made of fatty tissue. They also have throat pouches that allow them to make long calls that attract females.

FACTS

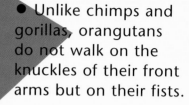

SIZE

● Unlike chimps and gorillas, orangutans do not walk on the knuckles of their front arms but on their fists.

● Their main predators are tigers.

DID YOU KNOW?

 Orangutans can grasp things with both their hands and feet.

 Unlike humans, orangutans have hips that are as flexible as their shoulders and arms.

 The word orangutan comes from the Malay language meaning "person of the forest."

Males and Females

▶ Males and females differ in size. Females can grow up to 4 ft. 2 in. (127 cm) and weigh around 100 lbs. (45.4 kg). Adult males can reach 5 ft. 9 in. (175 cm) in height and weigh over 260 lbs. (118 kg). A male's arm span is 6 ft. 6 in. (2 m). They have four fingers and a thumb that can grip.

Diet

▶ Orangutans mainly eat fruit, but they also eat vegetation, bark, honey, insects, and bird eggs.

Poison Dart Frog

Poison dart frogs are brightly colored to warn of their deadly nature. Only three species of poison dart frogs have the kind of poison that can kill humans. The poison oozes from their skin.

WHERE DO THEY LIVE?

In the rain forests of Central and South America and on a few Hawaiian islands.

Central America

South America

Leaping Frog

▶ The back legs have powerful muscles for jumping. They are not as athletic as some other frogs, though.

Deadly Frog

◀ A small, slow-moving animal, it eats poisonous insects, such as some ants. Then it concentrates the poison and stores it in special glands in the skin.

FACTS

SIZE

- Most poison dart frogs are brightly colored.

- A group of frogs is sometimes called an army.

- Poison dart frogs eat flies, crickets, ants, termites, and beetles.

DID YOU KNOW?

 Some poison dart frogs are endangered because of habitat loss.

 The amount of poison from a golden dart frog that is needed to kill a human is equal to 2–3 grains of table salt.

Also called poison arrow frogs because some Native American tribes have used the frog poison on their darts.

Catching Prey

▶ Each toe ends in a disc that is like a sucker. It lets the frog cling to slippery leaves and climb high into trees. The frog's mouth can open really wide to eat prey. The sticky tongue is attached to the front of the mouth, so it flips out a long way to catch insects and spiders.

Saltwater Crocodile

The saltwater crocodile is a giant among its kind. It is the world's largest living reptile. Some say it is the animal most likely to eat humans. It can live in salt water and swim huge distances between islands. They have often been spotted swimming far out at sea.

Speedy Croc

▶ Using powerful sweeps of its very long tail, the crocodile can swim at an extremely high speed.

WHERE DO THEY LIVE?

Asia

Southeastern Asia to northern Australia, New Guinea, and nearby Pacific Islands.

DID YOU KNOW?

 It senses vibrations in the ground through its jaw.

 The muscles used for closing the jaws are very powerful, but the muscles used for opening them are weak.

 Each back foot has four slim, webbed digits. The crocodile walks flat-footed on the full sole.

FACTS

- The world's largest living reptile.

- It is also one of the most dangerous reptiles.

- It can live up to 100 years or possibly longer.

SIZE

Man-Eater

◄ The saltwater crocodile hunts near the water's edge. If it grabs prey on land, the crocodile flings it or hauls it into the water, holds it underwater, and drowns it.

Replacement Teeth

► There are 64 to 68 teeth, which are widely spaced and pointed. These teeth are perfect for gripping but of no use for chewing or slicing. Each tooth is replaced by a new one as it wears out. The crocodile never loses its teeth as it gets older, which is one reason why it can live so long.

Siamese Fighting Fish

In the wild, these fish only show their bright colors when they are under threat. However, in captivity they have been bred so that they are always colorful. Males and females puff out their gill covers to impress each other.

Diet

▶ They are mainly carnivorous, feeding on zooplankton, crustaceans, and the larvae of mosquitoes and other insects.

WHERE DO THEY LIVE?

Asia

Originally native to the rice paddies of Thailand, Cambodia, and Malaysia in Asia.

DID YOU KNOW?

 In the wild, they only fight for a few minutes, but in captivity they have been bred to fight for much longer.

 The health of a Siamese fighting fish is shown by its color. The richer the color, the healthier it is.

 Females are duller in color and have shorter fins than males.

FACTS

SIZE

- They live for two to four years in captivity.

- They like water of around 77–86°F (25–30°C).

- Males can be very aggressive. It is better to keep them alone.

Reproduction

◀ Once the female has released all her eggs, she is chased away by the male because she might eat the eggs due to hunger. The male looks after the eggs.

Breathing

▶ Fish generally breathe through their gills, but Siamese fighting fish can also breathe in oxygen from the surface of the water. They do this through their labyrinth organ, which helps the oxygen be absorbed into the bloodstream.

Three-Toed Sloth

The three-toed sloth moves very slowly through the tropical forests of eastern Brazil. It has big hook claws, long arms, and a special coat that makes it well equipped for a life spent high in the trees. Surprisingly, it is also quite a good swimmer.

WHERE DO THEY LIVE?

Rain forests in South and Central America.

Central America

South America

Upside Down

▶ The three-toed sloth eats and sleeps while hanging upside down from tree branches.

DID YOU KNOW?

The sloth can hang from trees just by using its claws.

It can heal quickly when it is wounded. A wound is unlikely to become infected and will heal within two weeks.

Its slow-moving pace of life allows it to survive on a low-energy vegetarian diet.

FACTS

SIZE

● It relies on camouflage for protection.

● It is so used to life in the trees that it is awkward on the ground.

● Its diet is mainly leaves and buds.

Camouflage

◀ It is difficult to see a sleeping sloth. Its skin color and hairs blend in very well with the trees in which it sleeps.

Special Coat

▶ The thick hairs on the coat grow upward from a parting in the middle of the stomach toward the ridge of the spine. This allows rain to run off when the sloth is upside down. A blue-green algae covers the hairs on the sloth's thick coat, providing camouflage.

Glossary

camouflage – to conceal by blending in with the habitat

captivity – to be kept in enclosed area, such as a zoo, nature preserve, or as a pet.

crustacean – an arthropod with a toughened outer shell covering its body

dominant – having the most control and influence

endangered – the risk of no more of the species being alive

extinct – describing a species that no longer exists

ferocious – fierce and scary

habitat – the natural environment where an animal lives

mottled – having spots or patches of color

muzzle – the part of an animal's face that sticks out, such as its nose and jaw

offspring – the young that adult animals have given birth to

predator – animal that lives by killing other animals

prey – animals that are killed by other animals

rain forest – a thick, green forest with an high annual rainfall. Rain forests are often, but not always, in tropical regions.

roosting – when birds rest or sleep on a perch

reptile – a cold-blooded animal such as snakes, lizards, and dinosaurs

species – a group of related animals that look like one another and can breed among themselves, but are not able to breed with members of another species.

venom – a poisonous matter

Further Information:

Books

Franklin, Carolyn. *Rain Forest Animals.* Book House, 2014.

Greenaway, Theresa. *Jungle.* DK Publishing, Inc., 2004.

Hardyman, Robyn. *Apes and Monkeys.* Brown Bear Books, 2009.

Hibbert, Clare. *If You Were A Snake.* Smart Apple Media, 2014.

Rice, Bill. *Endangered Animals of the Jungle.* Teacher Created Materials, 2013.

Websites

http://www.allaboutwildlife.com/list-of-jungle-animals
Find out about endangered jungle animals

http://www.worldlandtrust.org/webcams
Discover life in the rain forest by watching live webcams

http://www.sciencekids.co.nz/sciencefacts/earth/jungles.html
Learn fascinating fun facts about jungle animals

http://www.junglephotos.com/africa/afanimals/afanimals.shtml
See up-close photos of jungle animals, presented with detailed information about each creature

Index: